words

A Highly Favoured Life Devotional

1st Edition published in 2023
2nd Edition published in 2025

ISBN:
978-1-967189-06-9
978-1-967189-07-6

Table of Contents

Dedication

This devotional is dedicated to the godly ladies God has
placed in our lives who have often passed on good words.
They not only passed along a good word but also gave us
words of admonition and encouragement
as we walked along life's way.

Introduction

"Word of Praise"
By Rachel Post

In times of trouble and distress,
I call upon Your name.
And without fail, You bring me rest
Or comfort just the same.

You take the time to plant my feet
Upon a solid place.
You shower me with mercy
And bathe me in Your grace.

Though I walk through darkest paths,
And my way seems bleak,
You wrap Your arms around me
In times when I am weak.

Every need you have supplied,
All my hopes fulfilled.
You walk with me, abide with me
And You always will.

I find new morning mercies
And delight in all You do,
Yet often go about my day
Without thanking You.

One would think with all you do
My lips would never cease
To praise and glorify Your name
And tell of my increase.

Even without my reply,
You do not change Your ways.
How sad the truth that days go by
Without a word of praise.

Written by one of our authors, this poem by Mrs. Rachel Post calls to attention one of the most important uses of our words — praise to our God. Her devotion begins our book to remind us to praise Him often for His might and power are beyond worthy!

Words of Praise

By Rachel Post

And call upon me in the day of trouble: I will deliver thee, and thou shalt glorify me.

Psalm 50:15

Have you ever found yourself in a situation that seemed completely hopeless? Have you looked around and found nobody who could truly understand how you were feeling? Your fleshly refuge had failed you. It seemed as though no man cared for your soul. (Psalm 142:4-7a, "I looked on my right hand, and beheld, but there was no man that would know me: refuge failed me; no man cared for my soul. I cried unto thee, O Lord: I said, Thou art my refuge and my portion in the land of the living. Attend unto my cry; for I am brought very low... Bring my soul out of prison, that I may praise thy name....")

Just as you felt that you were about to be pulled down permanently by life's current, you looked up. There it was, a hand extended to you — a warm embrace, a blanket of forgiveness and understanding, someone who not only listened to your complaints, but welcomed them —

(Psalm 142:2, "I poured out my complaint before him: I shewed before him my trouble.") the only Being Who was capable of changing your situation. Can you feel it? – the acceptance – the calm assurance that help is on the way? Maybe you cannot, because you have never experienced His rest.

You are thinking, "How can I reach Him? How can I solicit His help?" The answer, my friend, is much simpler than your problem. All you need to do is ask. Picture the Lord able to uplift and assist you; He is anticipating and longing to come to your aid, but is waiting for you to ask. Just as children need to ask their parents for help, we need to ask our Heavenly Father to extend His hand to us.

After He extends His hand to you and lifts you out of the waves, can you picture Him waiting there – waiting to be thanked – waiting to be praised? So often we are as the healed lepers who received their healing and never returned to thank the Healer. The Lord has saved our souls and our lives, and we neglect to take the time to praise Him. What a shame to think of all the help we receive, and how little we actually thank Him.

Psalm 62:8 "Trust in him at all times; ye people, pour out your heart before him: God is a refuge for us."

words

Thoughts:

Prayers:

Word Toolbox

By Catherine Aylor

*Who is a wise man and endued with knowledge among you? let him shew out
of a good conversation his works with meekness of wisdom.
But the wisdom that is from above is first pure, then peaceable, gentle, and easy to be
intreated, full of mercy and good fruits, without partiality, and without hypocrisy.*

James 3:13;17

Words are a powerful thing. James 3 speaks all about the tongue. It is a great chapter about getting our words under submission. Verse 5 says, "Even so the tongue is a little member, and boasteth great things. Behold, how great a matter a little fire kindleth!" Something so small has a great responsibility. Verse 10 goes on to say, "Out of the same mouth proceedeth blessing and cursing. My brethren, these things ought not so to be." How can blessings and cursing come from the same mouth?

I believe there are times in our life where we find ourselves "not knowingly or knowingly" using the wrong words. Words are those things that can never be taken back. Once they are out, it is like a crumpled piece of paper. You can open the paper back up and straighten it again, but there is no way to "iron out" all the wrinkles. It is so important we choose our words wisely inside and out. What is in our heart will spew from our mouths in different times of life. It is important to have words for everything we may go through. Kind of like a battle plan for life. We need to have a "word" toolbox for when we have things to face or to help others in things they may face. Let me share with you a few areas God has shown me where we may need to find the right words and where we can get them from – God's Word. James 3:13;17 tells us where words should come from and how they should be used. (Look up these verses as you receive the "tools" to make it through these times with the right words.)

Words for Waiting–Lamentations 3:25

God is good to those who wait on Him. It is not your timing. Waiting does not mean we sit around and just wait like a child who keeps asking, "Are we there, yet?" They go, sit, and sulk. It is about the ending of the verse "... to the soul that seeketh him." We should be waiting like a waitress. She comes and checks on you, serves you, refreshes you, and makes sure she does anything possible to make your experience the best. We need to be doing that for God. We need to be checking in with His Word, serving him while waiting, and refreshing others with our example.

Words of Wisdom–Psalm 111:10; Proverbs 9:10

These verses talk about the fear of the Lord being "the beginning of wisdom." This fear is a respect, not an "afraid" fear. This beginning of knowledge requires a few things as the verse says, "all they that do his commandments." The fear of the Lord is the beginning of knowledge, but the action part is the understanding. Proverbs 2:6 talks about when we begin with the "fear of the Lord," our words are going to come from our mouth to others as an example of knowledge and understanding of God at important times when wisdom is required.

Words to do His Work—Proverbs 14:23

We can talk and say we love the Lord, but talk only gets us "penury"—meaning in a poor, destitute state. Colossians 3:23-24 shows us how to work – everything heartily as unto the Lord. It is not for others, but for Him. He showed us the greatest example, and when His work was done, He said it well, "It is finished!" We have a very good reason to work as His finished work created our hope. We certainly do not work for salvation (Ephesians 2:8-9). We work because we are saved and for His honor and his glory.

Words for our Walk—II Corinthians 5:7-21

We walk by faith and not by sight. We need to be reminded to walk confidently, but because of God, not ourselves. This passage tells us how we can walk by faith. We can have this confidence and the words for all times during our walk because we are to be "absent from the body and present with the Lord." The Lord has made us new creatures in Him. Christ sees all, understands all, and can help us with anything we face. Dying to ourselves daily will help us be able to walk as if we are seated in heaven.

Words for the World—Romans 12:1-3

We have to live in this world, but we are not to be a part of the world. We are to be different, yet not thinking of ourselves as better than those of the world. We can do this by the "...renewing of our minds" with His words and Scripture. We are to be sober or serious about the things of God. The world is looking at us. When we are faced with battles like waiting, renewing our minds in Him will help build our faith, longsuffering, and patience. Our fruit will be evident allowing us growth in the future. Some are looking for answers and need us to help them with words of wisdom, not anger, gossip, and "what we think." The world is looking at our work and our walk.

"What we look like to the world is what will be evident when we fill or don't fill ourselves with HIS WORDS in this toolbox called life."

- Catherine Aylor

words

Thoughts:

Prayers:

Let the Words of My Mouth...

By Corli Hall

Let the words of my mouth, and the meditation of my heart,
be acceptable in thy sight, O Lord, my strength, and my redeemer.

Psalm 19:14

This is a verse I pray regularly because I need to! It comes as no surprise that the Bible makes frequent and diverse references to the little things we utter thousands of times a day – words! In fact, Scripture teaches us that our words contain the power of death and life! James 3:8 sheds light on just how dangerous they are: "But the tongue can no man tame; it is an unruly evil, full of deadly poison." It is easy to understand why our enemy would so often entice us to use our words for evil instead of good and why it is so difficult to control. Oh, to be better stewards of that which proceeds out of our mouth. Oh, to speak life and bring blessing with my words!

As with every discipline in the Christian life, we can take courage and know that, through the working and empowering of the Spirit, it is possible. As humbling as it is to accept our weakness regarding this subject and as daunting as the challenge to speak only acceptable words might be, we can be equally excited about the opportunities this challenge presents. There is hope for good and not evil with our words. However, it is a choice — a conscience decision that we make and re-make everyday. We must then rely on the Lord to do that good work in us.

It is a heart-discipline we exercise so that we may become trained and strong in speaking words that bring life and grace to the hearers. How do we overcome evil with good? By putting off that which is bad and replacing it with that which is good and acceptable to God. What are some things we can replace to ensure our words bring honor to God and life to the hearers? Here are few suggestions:

1. Replace gossip with prayer — Ephesians 4:29; Matthew 5:44.
2. Replace hatred with love — Luke 6:27-29.
3. Replace anger with grace — Colossians 4:6.
4. Replace bitterness with forgiveness. — Matthew 5:44.
5. Replace speaking with listening — Proverbs 21:23; Proverbs 13:3; James 1:19.
6. Replace pride with humility — Proverbs 13:10.
7. Replace complaining with encouragement — Philippians 2:14; Romans 15:1-2; Romans 15:5.
8. Replace slander with upliftment — Proverbs 10:18.
9. Replace indifference with determination — James 1:26.

"If you feel your tongue itch to talk nonsense, trace it to the devil, not to the Spirit of God!"

- Charles Spurgeon

Are my words true? Are they kind? Are they necessary?

words

Thoughts:

Prayers:

Speaking to Ourselves

By Tresa Barber

Finally, brethren, whatsoever things are true, whatsoever things are honest, whatsoever things are just, whatsoever things are pure, whatsoever things are lovely, whatsoever things are of good report; if there be any virtue, and if there be any praise, think on these things.

Philippians 4:8

It is important to God how we talk to ourselves! He specifically tells us what to think about because our thoughts will affect our words and our actions. Right thoughts do not always come to us automatically. We must make a conscience choice to think thoughts that please Him – and when we do, we will be blessed! Right thoughts will produce joy!

Ephesians 5:19 says, "Speaking to yourselves in psalms and hymns and spiritual songs, singing and making melody in your heart to the Lord;" The Word of God is powerful, and it affects our spirit when we recall Scripture. That's why we need to memorize Scripture so that it may readily come to our minds and help us. Singing spiritual songs confirms God's truth in our hearts. We may sing aloud or in our thoughts as we are working around the house, driving the car, or having an awake time in the middle of the night! Hymns about all of God's wonderful attributes can quiet our hearts as we remember our God is in control, and He sees us and is working for our good.

God also tells us what to think about when we are confronted with situations that confuse us, and we do not know what to do. We can be tempted to be very discouraged or depressed. When this happens, we need to check the words we think – all the thoughts that run through our minds – by Philippians 4:8. It says, "Finally, brethren, whatsoever things are true, whatsoever things are honest, whatsoever things are just, whatsoever things are pure, whatsoever things are lovely, whatsoever things are of good report; if there be any virtue, and if there be any praise, think on these things."

Situations, or even people, can seem hopeless, but we can choose to encourage ourselves in the Lord. David did that! When the wives and children of David's soldiers were taken captive while they were fighting a battle, everyone blamed David. I Samuel 30:6, "And David was greatly distressed; for the people spake of stoning him, because the soul of all the people was grieved, every man for his sons and for his daughters: but David encouraged himself in the LORD his God." How would David have encouraged himself? He would remind himself that God was watching and cared what happened to them; he would remember God's promises and claim them; he would recall other times when God worked on his behalf.

God cares about our words. He graciously offers His guidance so that we can please Him and have victory in this important matter! Thank you, Lord, for your provision for us!

words

Thoughts:

Prayers:

Our Words

By Makayla Fehr

Death and life are in the power of the tongue:
and they that love it shall eat the fruit thereof.

Proverbs 18:21

Most likely if you grew up in a Christian home, you constantly heard your mother say, "Think twice before you speak once." Now as an adult, that advice is more important than ever before! I have always liked using the illustration of a tube of toothpaste. The toothpaste is super easy to get out of the tube, but impossible to get it back in. The same goes for our words; once they are out of our mouth, we can never take them back. That is why we have to be so careful about what we say. As Christian ladies, I feel like there are some different ways we can use our words to be a blessing to others!

W— Wise (Proverbs 10:19 ; Ecclesiastes 10:12)

We always need to think before we speak, being wise in our response to people. It is so easy to just say the first thing that pops into our head, but those words would most likely not be words of wisdom. Praying every day that the Lord would fill you with His Holy Spirit and that He would give you the words to say and speak is of utmost importance.

O– Optimistic (1 Corinthians 14:26)

Having a good attitude and perspective on things is not always the easiest, but it is always best. You never know whose life you can change by being optimistic. Instead of always discouraging people and putting them down, be the kind of lady people can count on to bring the good out of any situation. Be someone they would love to go to for good words, especially when they need encouragement!

R– Respectful (Colossians 4:6)

Using our words to respect others and be respectful about other people is important. If you respect someone, show it and say it. It will earn their respect towards you.

D– Discreet (Titus 2:5)

As a youth pastor's wife, I am constantly reminding the young ladies that they need to be discreet in their speech. Ladies, we have a tendency to speak our mind in the heat of the moment and then regret it later. I do believe it is a lifetime process to learn to be discreet, but it is something we can work at every single day.

S– Sweet (Psalms 119:103; Proverbs 31:26)

We should want to be known as ladies who are always sweet with their words and always kind about others. I want to be known as a lady who is kind and sweet with her words, not always bashing and bringing other people down.

Just remember, once the words are out, they can never be put back, no matter how many times you apologize and truly mean it. So let us be ever so careful with our words!

words

Thoughts:

Prayers:

Acronyms of Choice

By Marie Barron

As for God, his way is perfect: the word of the Lord is tried:
he is a buckler to all them that trust in him.

II Samuel 22:31

Word acronyms help others understand what a word means to you. I am choosing three words and giving an acronym to show others what God has done and continues to do for me.

Love: **Lasting, Outstanding, Valuable, Enduring**

God has blessed my life in tremendous ways. I have always felt His love for me. When I was ten, my dad passed away leaving my mom to raise four children. During these difficult years, Mom allowed us children to ride the church bus to Calvary Baptist Church where I learned how much God loved me, all that Jesus had done for me, and my need to be saved (John 3:16).

Salvation: **Sustaining, Always, Longsuffering, Victorious, Amazing, Thankful, Incredible, Owner, Never-ending,**

I was saved on January 11,1971, at twelve years of age. Shortly after I was saved, my life and the world as I knew it changed again – a move into the city. At this time, I stopped going to my church, but I continued to go to a different church. The Lord continued to hold me in His protective arms, and despite my many mistakes, He never let go of me. As the years passed, I got married and started a family. Through those years, God used every word in my salvation acronym to help and guide me. I knew I needed to get back to Calvary. I began attending regularly, gave my heart totally back to God, and have tried to stay faithful ever since.

Faith: Father, Awesome, Interested, Trustworthy, Hugs/Holding

As my journey continues, my faith needs to be stronger than ever (Proverbs 3:5-6). My heavenly Father knew His plans for me and always proved Himself in all ways of my faith acronym. I was tried through many losses: babies, grandmother, siblings, my husband of forty-two years, and my momma. Never once did my Father let me go through these losses alone. During my greatest fears and heartaches, I felt the arms of God holding me. It was a very literal hug from God! Sometimes there are no words to comfort, just a hug is what is needed (Hebrews 10:23). (Side note: A widow misses physical hugs more than you know. God allowed me to become a Christian school teacher; my Kindergarten students have comforted me with plenty of hugs).

Often in my life, I have felt inadequate to serve in an area I was placed in to serve. As I prayed, God reminded me that I may not be worthy to serve, but I can be faithful. I pray with all my heart that God continues to keep me faithful and allows me to serve Him (II Corinthians: 5:10).

words

Thoughts:

Prayers:

Words of Contentment

By Anja Meyer

Not that I speak in respect of want: for I have learned, in whatsoever state I am, therewith to be content.

Philippians 4:11

As this is the first devotion I have written, I thought I would write a little introduction about myself.

I live in England, but I come from South Africa. All our family is in South Africa, and I miss them terribly! England is cold, gloomy and wet. What a contrast to the hot, sunny outdoor lifestyle I grew up with! Everything in England is small – the houses, gardens and roads. With six children and a large van to transport them, I often long for the wide South African roads, comfortable houses, and huge gardens. Homeschooling these same children is quite the task! It is exhausting and never having a break is probably the most tiresome thing for mum. I recently lost my unborn son and my dear mum in close succession. These were the hardest things I have had to go through on this earth so far. I felt I still wanted so many years and memories with them!

Determine to use words of contentment even if you do not feel like it.

Did this quick bio leave a heaviness and even an unpleasantness in your heart? Did it convey feelings of depression and negativity? It was all true, but the way I used my words caused discontentment instead of bringing glory to the LORD. Let me try again.

My family and I come from South Africa, but we have a wonderful opportunity to serve the Lord in England. What a joy to be involved in the publishing and distribution of Hebrew Scriptures! I am thankful that we get to see my family about every other year, and enjoy wonderful holidays with them in sunny South Africa. The weather in England is quite mild, so we do not have tons of snow like mainland Europe. The Lord has blessed us with six children, a dependable van, beautiful house, and larger-than-average garden for them to enjoy. It is such a privilege to be able to spend all day with these children, teaching them and training these hearts who look up to me and love me without restrictions. While exhausting at times, the Lord is faithful to provide the strength I need. I also have a precious son with the Lord! I cannot wait to meet him in Heaven and spend eternity with him serving our wonderful Saviour. My dear mum recently also went to be with the Lord. I am so thankful for the wonderful mum I had, and all that she taught me to be a good wife and mother. I am looking forward to seeing her again someday too!

It is my prayer that these words brought encouragement, hope, and honor to the LORD. It is all true too, the flip side of the coin, simply stated from a different perspective – contentment.

Our words bring out certain things in our own hearts, but also in the hearts of those who hear us. In my case, it is mostly my husband and children that hear my words. Will they feel joy and be encouraged in their walk with the Lord when they daily hear my words? Will my words bring them hope and build their faith? As a wife and mother, your words will determine the atmosphere of your home.

The old hymn, "Count Your Blessings," often comes to my mind. It reminds us to count our blessings, to name them one by one. The Lord is so, so good to us. We should focus on these blessings. We should think about these, but more importantly, we should speak about them.

It really boils down to contentment. When you are content, it will bubble out of your heart in your words to bless others and build their contentment. Philippians 4:11 says, "Not that I speak in respect of want: for I have learned, in whatsoever state I am, therewith to be content." I Timothy 6:6, "But godliness with contentment is great gain."

Ask the LORD to work contentment in your heart. Get an accountability partner to gently indicate to you when your usage of words moves away from contentment. And be encouraged, dear sister: Philippians 4:19-20, "But my God shall supply all your need according to his riches in glory by Christ Jesus. Now unto God and our Father be glory for ever and ever. Amen."

(For further reading and studying on this topic, I highly recommend Ephesians 5, where it mentions giving thanks in both verse 4 and verse 20.)

words

Thoughts:

Prayers:

Speech Delays

By Alicia Moss

...but I am slow of speech, and of a slow tongue.

Exodus 4:10

Speech? Speech can be the expression of or the ability to express thoughts and feelings by articulating sounds. How do you speak? Is your speech purposeful and godly? Matthew 12:36 says, "... every idle word that men shall speak, they shall give account thereof in the day of judgment."

Not many weeks ago, our family was coming home from church when our three-year-old kept hollering at the top of his lungs. He was not crying or whining; he was trying to communicate with us. My husband wisely did not rebuke him, but asked him, "Park, Park, do you have trouble saying your words?" He responded with "uh-huh" before falling to silence for the next fifteen minutes of our car ride. His silence broke our hearts, and we have decided to look outside our home for the help that he needs.

Through this experience, I have discovered there are many factors that can hinder the development of speech. Even Moses felt that his speech was not adequate for ministering and leading others. Exodus 4:10 "... but I am slow of speech, and of a slow tongue." Do you have a spiritual speech delay? One component of being labeled speech delayed is the level of our receptive language or our ability to understand language. How do you understand our God's great language, the Bible? Maybe your words are not holy, godly, and praising because you have no understanding of His language. Look deep in your heart. Maybe salvation is what you need. Do you hear His voice when you read His words? Do you hear His voice in those quiet times? John 10:4 "... and the sheep follow him: for they know his voice." If you are accustomed to hearing His voice, speaking his language will become natural. If you are unfamiliar with His voice, you will not speak language that honors our Savior.

Another component of having a speech delay is the level of ability to hear. Difficulty in hearing significantly impacts the ability to speak, use language, and understand others. Are your ears clogged with the "wax" of this world? Maybe you do not actively and consistently listen to His voice. Maybe your "hearing aid" is not turned up. How much focus do you devote to hearing His voice? Going to church three times a week and revival services is great, however hearing and talking to our Savior must be done in private as well. Ladies, let us decide to grab our "hearing aids," clean out the "wax" of this world, and get to know His Word. If we know His Word, our speech will glorify and honor Him.

I challenge you to grow in your speech. Do not be as Moses was, making excuses for your possible speech delay. Exodus 4:12, "Now therefore go, and I will be with thy mouth, and teach thee what thou shalt say." The Lord will guide our speech, but we must actively listen to His Word and practice speaking His words.

Questions to Ponder:
- Do you have a spiritual speech delay?
- What is causing your speech to be delayed?
- How could you improve your speech?

words

Thoughts:

Prayers:

Let the Words of My Mouth

By Rita Nichols

Let the words of my mouth, and the meditation of my heart,
be acceptable in thy sight, O Lord, my strength, and my redeemer.

Psalms 19:14

David the psalmist wrote in Psalms 19:14, "Let the words of my mouth, and the meditation of my heart, be acceptable in thy sight, O Lord, my strength, and my redeemer." I believe that this was a prayer that he made to God. David desired to be so in tune with the Lord that he wanted nothing to come between him and God.

Firstly, David asked that his words be acceptable. He wanted everything that came out of his mouth to not only please God, but also glorify the Lord.

Secondly, David recognized that the problem was not just his mouth, but it was a problem of the heart. The words that we say are a result of the things that we have allowed our hearts to entertain. The Apostle Paul wrote to the church in Philippi in Philippians 4:8, "Finally, brethren, whatsoever things are true, whatsoever things are honest, whatsoever things are just, whatsoever things are pure, whatsoever things are lovely, whatsoever things are of good report; if there be any virtue, and if there be any praise, think on these things." Paul's instructions reveal that it is important to keep our thoughts on the correct things. Proverbs 23:7a says, "For as he thinketh in his heart, so is he...." David wanted God to dig deeper into the very root of his words.

Lastly, our words are just the symptom of our heart problem. Many times as we get older, we lose that ability to filter our speech, and often those bitter and angry thoughts just come spewing out. If we could simply keep our thoughts on the Lord, then we would be like the Proverbs 31 woman, "She openeth her mouth with wisdom; and in her tongue is the law of kindness (v. 26)"

words

Thoughts:

Prayers:

Careless Words

By Crystal Aldridge

Set a watch, O LORD, before my mouth; keep the door of my lips.

Psalm 141:3

Careless words often cause hurt and pain unintentionally. Phrases such as "think before you speak" and "choose your words wisely" serve as cautionary reminders that we should be careful with our words! The expression "careless" means not giving sufficient attention or thought to avoid harm or errors. We cannot put careless words back once we spew them out of our mouths.

I vividly remember sitting in a fast-food restaurant as a child when a family member criticized my appearance. It was not something I could change, like a dirty face or messy hair. That day, the words spoken to me provoked self-deprecating thoughts I had never had before. That was not this person's intention. Sadly, this happens too often. The Bible says in James 3:5, "Even so the tongue is a little member, and boasteth great things. Behold, how great a matter a little fire kindleth!"

Identifying a gossiping or slandering tongue is not tricky. It is easy to recognize backbiting and whispering. Yet, often we attempt to justify or excuse words spoken carelessly by saying things like, "I didn't mean it that way," or "I was only joking." Matthew 12:36 says we will give an account for every idle word. It does not matter the excuse we offer. I cannot tame my tongue (James 3:8), but I know Who can.

I often pray the prayer David prayed in Psalm 141:3, "Set a watch, O LORD, before my mouth; keep the door of my lips." Lord, please help me guard my tongue! I want to be thoughtful and gracious with my words.

We cannot put careless words back once we spew them out of our mouths.

words

Thoughts:

Prayers:

The Tongue

By Judy Rolfe

The Lord God hath given me the tongue of the learned, that I should know how to speak a word in season to him that is weary....

Isaiah 50:4

Words. I like words. Words can be fun. Scrabble is the word game that our family enjoys. Our granddaughter recently informed us that she was expecting her first baby by placing words on a Scrabble board. I was also recently introduced to Wordle by my son. Now we have a family group that competes daily.

Words can also be helpful. As a teacher of forty-one years, I have learned the importance of knowing the meanings of words. Children will ask every time a new word is introduced. Oftentimes, a sentence needs just that perfect word to sound complete.

We also know that words can cut like a knife. Criticism, negativism, and harsh words destroy friendships, marriages, and families. Our words can truly make or ruin someone else's day. The Bible says much about the tongue and our inability to control it. Some have said that our teeth are bars to keep our tongue from getting away from us. Job 38:2 speaks of "dark counsel" because words were used without knowledge.

As Christians, our words should honor and glorify and praise the Lord. The words of our songs should be honoring to Him. We should use our words to praise and thank Him for all He does for us. We glorify Him when we use our words to testify of His saving grace and tell others how they can be ready to go to heaven when they die.

In our verse, God gave Isaiah the tongue of the learned so he would know how to speak and when his words would be appropriate. We, too, can seek this wisdom from God Almighty, and he will grant it. Please remember—we can make or break someone else's day by what we say. When we have God's wisdom, our words will bring comfort, encouragement, and help when it is most needed. Let's keep our words sweet—and fun!

words

Thoughts:

Prayers:

I Want to Give Life

By Marsha Leto

Death and life are in the power of the tongue:
and they that love it shall eat the fruit thereof.

Proverbs 18:21

Words are the most powerful tool we have as Christian ladies. The right words can encourage, heal, and help. Kind words can give life to someone who has lost hope.

When I was ten years old, my dad promised me that he would pick me up from school. I waited and waited, but he never came. That day was a very traumatic day for me, and one that I will never forget. I was so confused and hurt. I had many questions for my mom. My mom said we could talk, but first we needed to get a Frosty from Wendy's. I think she was giving herself time to process the event that had taken place that day. I remember being very excited about going to the new restaurant in town, Wendy's. The Frosty was delicious! After we finished the Frosty, my mom explained to me that my Dad was not coming back. He had left our family for another family. The tears flowed that day and for many days and years after that.

Another thing that I remember about that day was my mom telling me she loved me and that we were going to get through this together. She

57

said that the Lord had always taken care of us, and He would continue to do so. Before we left the restaurant, we prayed together and asked the Lord to help my mom find a job and to work in my dad's life. After our time at Wendy's, I honestly do not ever remember being scared about not having my dad in my life. Do not get me wrong, I missed my dad terribly, but I was not scared that Mom could not take care of us. There were a lot of changes we went through in that first year, but I was secure because of my mom's words to me on that day and many days after that.

Here are some things I feel my mom said right that helped me so much.

She expressed unconditional love all the time.

She never bad-mouthed my dad. She would get quiet and say nothing but never ranted about how bad he was.

She spoke about how God gives a peace that passeth all understanding (Philippians 4:7).

She said I could do anything God wanted me to do.

She used her words to support the authorities in our life, even though her authority had betrayed her.

She used her words to give people the benefit of the doubt.

She made me want to have a relationship with the Lord because she talked about how good God is.

We really do not know what people are going through around us. Let us decide that we will try to give life to our circle of influence.

What positive things can I say to someone around me today?

words

Thoughts:

Prayers:

Wonderful Words of Life

By Breanna Patton

Let the words of my mouth, and the meditation of my heart,
be acceptable in thy sight, O Lord, my strength, and my redeemer.

Psalm 19:14

O generation of vipers, how can ye, being evil, speak good things?
for out of the abundance of the heart the mouth speaketh.

Matthew 12:34

What kind of words are you speaking today? Do you ever find yourself speaking critical, mean, and hurtful words? I know that I do. Who often takes the brunt of these words? Your husband? Your kids? Your friends or family? These are the people in our lives that we should be encouraging and uplifting with our words. Let's look at some reasons why we may be saying the words that we do.

First of all, what kind of things are you thinking and dwelling on? Are they things that are moral, good, righteous, or are they discouraging and critical? The Psalmist says in Psalm 19:14, "Let the words of my mouth, and the meditations of my heart, be acceptable in thy sight, O Lord, my strength, and my redeemer." Our desire should be that our words are acceptable to our Heavenly Father. Maybe there are some things in our

61

lives that we are thinking about and dwelling on that we should replace with memorized scripture passages, listening to preaching, or Christian podcasts. I find personally that if there is something I need to get out of my life, the only way I can really get rid of that thing is to replace it with something God-honoring.

Second of all, what kinds of things are you reading – in book form, social media, or other reading materials? If there is someone you follow on social media that is always being critical and putting others down, soon you may start incorporating critical words into your vocabulary. We have to, especially as ladies, be so careful of what we consume through social media. So many things that we see and hear through social media can cause us to be discontent in where God has us and what we have. If these negative reading materials are what we are dwelling on, it will eventually come out through our words. Matthew 12:34b says, "...for out of the abundance of the heart the mouth speaketh."

Christian lady, what is in your heart today? What is coming out of your mouth on a daily basis? I will leave you with this thought – every word that you speak will either damage or uplift. What kind of words will you speak today?

words

Thoughts:

Prayers:

Waiting and Working Words

By Hope Reimers

Let the words of my mouth, and the meditation of my heart,
be acceptable in thy sight, O Lord, my strength, and my redeemer.

Psalm 19:14

Words are effective no matter what type of personality you have. A person's reputation or testimony can definitely affect the weight of a person's words, but every spoken and written word is effective in some way.

Actions do speak louder than words, but words, more often than not, are the puppeteers of those actions. Everything we say has a consequence. My husband tells students all the time that they can choose what they do, but they cannot choose the consequences of it. It is so easy to speak absentmindedly through everyday life, but we need to realize that our words do carry weight.

Proverbs 26:20-21 states, "Where no wood is, there the fire goeth out: so where there is no talebearer, the strife ceaseth. As coals are to burning coals, and wood to fire; so is a contentious man to kindle strife." In my elementary classroom, we have been talking about forms of energy in science. One sub-topic is about waiting and working energy. Anything that has the potential for energy, such as firewood or coal, is called waiting energy. Working energy is what happens when firewood and coal are burned and give off light and heat.

In this verse, the potential of that firewood is gossip. When the kindling of gossip is used, it turns into working energy that burns and fuels strife. If that wood or coal is not used, the strife never starts to burn. The potential is always there, but we choose how often it is used.

Proverbs 16:24 states, "Pleasant words are as an honeycomb, sweet to the soul, and health to the bones." The "waiting energy" of our words can have the healing potential of honey rather than the destructive potential of firewood and coal. Its "working energy" power could fuel encouragement and strength to those around us. If those pleasant words are not used, healing, encouragement, and strength will not happen. The potential is always there, but we choose how often it is used.

Psalm 19:14 says, "Let the words of my mouth, and the meditation of my heart, be acceptable in thy sight, O Lord, my strength, and my redeemer." All words start with inner thoughts. If our thought life is what it ought to be, our words will have the right effect on those around us.

Language and spoken words are beautiful, God-given gifts. We have the liberty to use them in any way we choose. What kind of waiting energy do your thoughts and words possess? What actions and scenarios do you want your words to be responsible for today?

words

Thoughts:

Prayers:

Let My Words Be Sweet

By Sarah Russell

The thoughts of the wicked are an abomination to the LORD:
but the words of the pure are pleasant words.

Proverbs 15:26

Pleasant words are as an honeycomb,
sweet to the soul, and health to the bones.

Proverbs 16:24

As a child, I often heard this repeated, "If you can't say anything nice, don't say anything at all." I think it is a phrase by which even adults should live their lives. The Bible speaks in many verses about the effects our words have on others. Good and bad, words can cause hurtful wounds. Words can cheer and even bring good health! Imagine if the only words you ever heard from a loved one were negative – beating down, belittling, and discouraging you. You would feel poorly about yourself all the time, wouldn't you? But we would feel pretty good if our husband, parents, friends, and family constantly spoke words of encouragement, joy, and pleasantness into our lives! We would all do well to remember that our own words have the same effect on others!

Proverbs 15:26b says, "...the words of the pure are pleasant words." Are we living our everyday lives in such purity that the only words that come out are pleasant? According to Proverbs 16:24, pleasant words bring sweetness to the soul and even health to your very bones! Imagine that! You can make someone fell better physically with just your words. On the other hand, negative words can bring someone down, not only emotionally, but physically. So let's check our speech! Is it pleasant or negative? We could all do with a little more pure, pleasant conversation in the world we live in today. Don't you think? We need to be aware of the words coming out of our mouths. Do not let your words be foolish and meaningless. Let's speak pleasantly and positively with the direct purpose of encouragement and building up others in the Lord! You may speak sweet encouragement to the very soul of someone today; so be conscious of your words and their effect.

Father, please help my words today to be words of a pleasant nature to everyone I encounter along the way. Let me say as the Psalmist said, "Keep my tongue from evil, and thy lips from speaking guile" (34:13). Help me to keep my heart and mind pure so that "no corrupt communication will proceed out of my mouth" (Eph. 4:29-32). Teach me to speak truth and love into the hearts of everyone I meet. Sinner and saint – let them hear Your words of life coming from my unworthy lips today. In Jesus' name I pray, Amen.

words

Thoughts:

Prayers:

What Is The Fruit Of Your Words?

By Tricia Wood

Death and life are in the power of the tongue:
and they that love it shall eat the fruit thereof.

Proverbs 18:21

It is amazing how much the wisest man that ever lived had to say about our mouth, lips, tongue, and words. The book of Proverbs is full of instruction concerning these small but powerful members. Solomon tells us in this verse that the fruit of our tongue can yield death or can yield life. We are warned that we will have to eat the fruit of our tongue. What fruit do I prefer? One that brings death, or one that brings life?

How can I assure that my words bring life?

Galatians 5:22-23, "But the fruit of the Spirit is love, joy, peace, longsuffering, gentleness, goodness, faith, meekness, temperance: against such there is no law." It takes a daily yielding of myself to the Holy Spirit. If I am filled with the Holy Spirit, His fruit will come out in my words. As we run this race set before us, the devil, the world, and the flesh continually assault us. Therefore, I must also continue to yield myself to Him throughout the day. Those times I choose to live by the flesh, my words are filled with fleshly fruit.

Colossians 3:8 says, "But now ye also put off all these; anger, wrath, malice, blasphemy, filthy communications out of your mouth." Even though our tongue is a little member, it sure can create a large mess in a hurry.

Psalm 19:14 "Let the words of my mouth, and the meditation of my heart, be acceptable in thy sight, O Lord, my strength, and my redeemer." Lord, help my words to be filled with love, kindness, encouragement, gentleness, and praise. Help me to refrain from speaking words of gossip, backbiting, criticism, wrath, and strife. May the fruit of my words bring life!

We are warned that we will have to eat the fruit of our tongue.

words

Thoughts:

Prayers:

Choose Your Words Wisely

By Kay Reese

A word fitly spoken is like apples of gold in pictures of silver.

Proverbs 25:11

Words can make or break! They can send forth the truth, give encouragement, love, and praise. Sadly, words can also spread hurt, lies, hatred, and destruction.

When I was a child, we would say, "Sticks and stones may break my bones, but words will never hurt me." If only that were true! Unfortunately, there have been many times words have done much more harm than help. Another ole' saying we do not hear much anymore is, "If you cannot say anything nice, then just do not say anything at all!" Each of us must acknowledge that we have been guilty of speaking a word out of place.

Only God can help us to direct our words carefully. He desires for us to speak with truth, simplicity, kindness, and compassion. Everyone appreciates a kind word; a compliment. It will make their day much brighter. Proverbs 16:24 talks about our words being like a honeycomb—"sweet to the soul, and health to the bones."

Proverbs 15:23 declares, "A man hath joy by the answer of his mouth: and a word spoken in due season, how good is it!" We certainly can be grateful for those we have had the privilege to meet along life's journey who have passed a word of truth to us from the Lord. They opened their mouths to give us advice, letting us know by the way they spoke that they love us and understood our struggles. They sympathized with us and the burdens we carried upon our shoulders. Their words were priceless, giving us strength to go on.

Our words should be seasoned with the grace of our Almighty Father. He can give us the ability to choose our words for His honor and glory. The Bible says we will give an account for every idle word in Matthew 12:36. This is a great responsibility! Words can allow others to know what truly is in our hearts.

A queen called a very cruel woman into her presence. The queen asked the woman a question about the cruel words she had. The queen warned the woman that the answer she gave could send her into exile, banishing her from the kingdom! The queen looked at her, spoke firmly, and said, "Choose your words wisely."

Today, and every day, may we seek with the help of our Lord to do just that!

words

Thoughts:

Prayers:

Acceptable Words in His Sight

By Janna Buettner

Let the words of my mouth, and the meditation of my heart,
be acceptable in thy sight, O Lord, my strength, and my redeemer.

Psalm 19:14

Remember the children's chorus we learned as a child in Sunday school and junior church?–

> Oh, be careful little mouth what you say.
>
> Oh, be careful little mouth what you say.
>
> For the Father up above is looking down in love;
>
> Oh, be careful little mouth what you say.

Romans 12:1 instructs believers to "...present your bodies a living sacrifice, holy, acceptable unto God, which is your reasonable service." I Corinthians 6:19-20 says, "What? know ye not that your body is the temple of the Holy Ghost which is in you, which ye have of God, and ye are not your own? For ye are bought with a price: therefore glorify God in your body, and in your spirit, which are God's."

"Let the words of
my mouth, and
the meditation of
my heart, be
acceptable in thy
sight, O Lord,
my strength, and
my redeemer."
Psalm 19:14

Our mouth is a very small part of our body. We are the "temple"—the dwelling place of the Holy Ghost. We are to be acceptable unto God which is just our reasonable service. Our mouth and the words we say are to be acceptable to the Lord.

The book of James admonishes us to bridle our words, and in so doing, we are also able to bridle the whole body (James 3:2b, 5-6, 8, 10-11). The words that we say are simply an outpouring of what's in our heart. Matthew 12:34b-37 says, "...for out of the abundance of the heart the mouth speaketh. A good man out of the good treasure of the heart bringeth forth good things: and an evil man out of the evil treasure bringeth forth evil things. But I say unto you, That every idle word that men shall speak, they shall give account thereof in the day of judgment. For by thy words thou shalt be justified, and by thy words thou shalt be condemned."

The Lord wants us to walk in the spirit and let His mind be in us when we talk (Philippians 2:5; Proverbs 31:26; Proverbs 25:11). "Let no corrupt communication proceed out of your mouth, but that which is good to the use of edifying, that it may minister grace unto the hearers. And grieve not the holy Spirit of God, whereby ye are sealed unto the day of redemption. Let all bitterness, and wrath, and anger, and clamour, and evil speaking, be put away from you, with all malice: And be ye kind one to another, tenderhearted, forgiving one another, even as God for Christ's sake hath forgiven you" (Ephesians 4:29-32).

When we say hurtful words, we can be forgiven, but those words will never be forgotten. It is like going to the top of the Empire State Building and releasing thousands of feathers from a pillow and then trying to retrieve them all back. It is impossible. Every morning, we need to commit our hearts, minds, and mouths to the Lord so that we will be Christlike in the words out of our mouth and thoughts that come from our heart.

Jonathan Edwards said, "Resolved, never to do anything which I should be afraid to do if it were the last hour of my life." Our motto should be, "Resolved, never to say anything which I should be afraid to say if it were the last hour of my life."

words

Thoughts:

Prayers:

The Weight of Words

By Callie Payne

There is that speaketh like the piercings of a sword:
But the tongue of the wise is health.

Proverbs 12:18

Are you breaking down or building up? When others are around you, do they feel contention or comfort? Are you overflowing with envy or encouragement? When fellowshipping with friends, is your conversation positive or petty? What tone are you using? Do people walk away from your talks feeling refreshed by your words? Or do they walk away needing a major recharge because of the draining topic of negative conversation?

Why is it that we can get so offended or hurt over a short, hurtful conversation? Because words carry weight. They stick with you. I read a quote that said, "Be careful with your words. Once they are said, they can only be forgiven not forgotten." This is referring to negative and hurtful words. But positive words have weight too!

My elementary teacher used to say, "If you can't say something nice, don't say anything at all." It's a great day when you realize that sometimes it's okay not to speak, even if you have an opinion or something you

87

think may be worth adding to the conversation. I Thessalonians 4:11 says, "And that ye study to be quiet..." For shy ladies, being quiet comes a little more naturally than it does for us talkative ladies. Challenge yourself to study to just be quiet sometimes!

I cannot truthfully say that I've mastered this topic of weighing my words. Let's look at what the Bible says about the different words we choose to speak — because it is a choice. We often hear the statement "think before you speak." How often do we actually do that though? It's easy when the conversation is moving quickly to just misspeak and keep it moving. But those words are impossible to get back. Proverbs 27:17 says, "Iron sharpeneth iron; So a man sharpeneth the countenance of his friend." Are your words sharpening (strengthening) others? Or are your words cutting down others?

John 15:17 says, "These things I command you, that ye love one another." Romans 12:10 tells us to prefer one another. Sometimes we can be so quick to make a remark and let everyone know exactly what we are thinking — not stopping to think about the effects. Is it an asset to a conversation? Or is it even true at all? Words can make or break someone's day. Let's make sure we are speaking loving, unselfish, and kind words to our family, peers, coworkers, and church family.

What you are pondering in your heart will come out in the way you talk to and about those around you. Matthew 12:34b says, "For out of the abundance of the heart the mouth speaketh." We should strive to be ladies that prefer one another. Allow the weight of your words to reflect Christ with every conversation.

words

Thoughts:

Prayers:

The Fruit of Your Words

By Debra Birner

*Be ye therefore followers of God, as dear children; And walk in love,
as Christ also hath loved us, and hath given himself for us an offering
and a sacrifice to God for a sweetsmelling savour. But fornication,
and all uncleanness, or covetousness, let it not be once named among you,
as becometh saints; Neither filthiness, nor foolish talking, nor jesting,
which are not convenient: but rather giving of thanks.*

Ephesians 5:1-4

Early on in our Christian life, shortly after my husband became a deacon, we were invited to a fellowship party that consisted of the church's deacons and their wives, along with the Pastor and his wife. We were, at that time, still in a Southern Baptist church. We were humbled and excited to be able to attend this event with the leaders of our church, eager to learn and follow their example. Throughout the evening we sat and listened as the husbands and wives poked "fun" at each other constantly, laughing as they continually put each other down publicly. I was embarrassed for them.

On our way home, my husband looked at me and said, "I would never talk about you like that, especially in public." I felt so honored and safe as I knew I would never be put to such a public shame in the name of sport.

91

My husband and I do not joke around (jesting) about things that are holy. Our marriage relationship is holy. We watch what we say to each other and about each other. When we first got married, we made a predetermined decision to never discuss divorce, not even in joking. We declared we would not talk about the "D" word, as we referred to it.

My thirty-nine year old daughter recently recounted to me that as she was disciplining her own daughter, she suddenly recalled when I was angry with my children, I would walk around the house muttering, "I love my children. I love my children." Though everyone in the house at that time understood I was feeling more frustrated than loving, it was a good reminder to me at the time that, yes, I love my children, in spite of what the current circumstance may have been.

The next time you are tempted to jest, to just "joke around," or maybe blurt out something in anger, try implementing some thanksgiving and praise. Decades later, I am thankful for the times I did.

Proverbs 18:21 says, "Death and life are in the power of the tongue: and they that love it shall eat the fruit thereof."

words

Thoughts:

Prayers:

A Soft Answer

By Grace Shiflett

A soft answer turneth away wrath: but grievous words stir up anger.

Proverbs 15:1

Recently, someone came to my house needing advice about a very personal situation. I could tell the lady was braced for things to get heated, expecting me to answer her in the same tone that she was using toward me. As the conversation progressed, I purposed to do my best to defuse her hostility by responding with a soft answer. She did not expect that! A few minutes into the conversation, I saw the firmness in her countenance and her tone of voice slowly change. By the end of our chat, she and I were both smiling. After she left my house, I thought, "How I wish I would always try to respond with a soft answer and not grievous words."

So many times, we could avoid major conflicts if we would just choose to respond with soft words. Tender words do not always come easy but when they do come, the outcome can leave us with little to no regret.

From time to time, we will be faced with situations in life that can quickly be resolved if we would live by this verse – Proverbs 15:1.

When times of conflict come your way, ask the Lord to help you get into the habit of learning to control your words. It is not worth ruining the evening with your family, creating more conflict in your church or ministry, or causing friendships to be strained. A wise man once said, "You are the master of your words until they are spoken; then, they become the master of you." Purpose in your heart with the Lord's help to choose a soft answer. You will be glad you did!

So many times, we could avoid major conflicts if we would just choose to respond with soft words.

words

Thoughts:

Prayers:

A Word Fitly Spoken: Tools or Weapons?

By Christina Weems

A word fitly spoken is like apples of gold in pictures of silver.

Proverbs 25:11

The first verse the Lord brought to my mind with the topic of words was Proverbs 25:11. This phrase kept running through my mind – "a word fitly spoken...." How many times have we "stuck our foot in our mouth" or let words slip out before thinking? Honestly, this happens more times than we care to admit. God smote my heart with this thought: If spoken in the right time or manner, my words can be as beautiful as golden apples in silver frames. My speech can gracefully reflect that I am Christ's child, but I must allow Him to guide my thoughts so that I speak them in the timely manner He desires (Proverbs 15:23). Proverbs 18:21 says, "death and life are in the power of the tongue." Our speech can be used for two drastically different purposes: development or destruction.

Proverbs 16:24 tells us that "pleasant words are as an honeycomb, sweet to the soul, and health to the bones." Words can be developmental tools in two ways: edification and encouragement. Edify simply means "to instruct or improve someone morally or intellectually."

1 Thessalonians 5:11 and Romans 14:19 tell us to comfort and edify one another. Although edification is needful, we must acknowledge that it could come across as criticism, jealousy, or pride if not "fitly spoken." Therefore, with edification, allow God to guide us with a pure heart and a pleasant spirit.

Secondly, our words should be that tool of encouragement – giving hope, support, or confidence to one in need. We have all seen fellow Christians, whether struggling with loss, heartache, or loneliness, who would appreciate our uplifting words. Hebrews 3:13 says, "...exhort one another daily...." Allow God to use your words to develop and build up others.

In the same way that "fitly spoken" words can be a tool, those not fitly spoken can be a weapon of mass destruction. Essentially, our words can tear down others through two means: bitterness and backbiting. Proverbs 15:1 says that "...grievous words stir up anger." Anger is defined as "a strong feeling of displeasure or hostility" and can easily turn to bitterness in someone if left untreated. Be careful of the tone and intent of your words towards others. Backbiting or gossip, which is speaking badly of someone not present, can fabricate our words into harsh weapons. Gossip hurts and destroys others, which God relays to us in Proverbs 11:9 and 18:8. Proverbs 16:28 says "...a whisperer separateth chief friends." Psalm 34:13 admonishes us to "Keep...thy lips from speaking guile." With your words, seek to build relationships not break them.

One last verse that can encourage a "fitly spoken" word is this: "Let the words of my mouth, and the meditation of my heart, be acceptable in thy sight, O Lord, my strength, and my redeemer." (Psalm 19:14). Ask God to help your words lift up, not blow up!

words

Thoughts:

Prayers:

Post-It Note Challenge

By Christy Tadlock

Death and life are in the power of the tongue....

Proverbs 18:21

*As we have therefore opportunity, let us do good unto all men,
especially unto them who are of the household of faith.*

Galatians 6:10

Have you ever been weary in well doing? I have. Have you ever thought, does anybody even care or notice what I am doing? I have. Have you ever received encouragement from one little slip of paper? I have! Some of the greatest encouragement I have ever received has come from a simple note left on the organ, piano, and church pew.

"Just wanted you to know we love you! LeAnne." At the time I received this note, it honestly did not really faze me. I was in my teens and super excited about the opportunities I had to serve in my church. So, I just stuck it in my Bible. Over the last twenty years, I have come across the note multiple times during my devotions, and every time I find it, a syringe of "continue" is shot into my veins. This one little note reminds me that I have been serving far too long and too hard to give anything less than my best now.

"I love you and appreciate all the hard work you do! Victoria." This is ointment being applied to a tired mind when weary in well doing. My service is not unnoticed, it matters. When I've had thoughts of departing from "all-in," constant service, God manages to let me come across this little note I received, and it pumps life into me to continue on.

"Thank you so much for using your talents for the Lord. Love you!" It is a double shot iced macchiato or a sip of red bull to weary hands. In times of personal darkness or in a dry season as a church body, God will place this sticky-note in my path. A note cheering me on to continue through darkness and dryness until the next season comes.

Yes, I know we do not serve for the appreciation or benefit of others. We serve God. We play, sing, and teach for our Lord. But let's be real – darkness comes to every believer. Trials come to every faithful church member. Every church pianist or sound coordinator faces times of routine, where serving is a task to be done and not a joy. That is when they need it. They need a head-on collision with encouragement.

Do you encourage others through written words? You can speak words of encouragement; that is awesome. But honestly, spoken words can be easily forgotten. But written words? When saved by the receiver, they give life for years. Can God use you to write a note that gives life? I challenge you to buy a pack of sticky notes, jot a sentence of encouragement down, and leave it on a church pew. Leave it on a piano bench. Leave it in a sound booth. Life is in the very words you write on that note!

words

Thoughts:

Prayers:

An Encouraging Word

By Hannah Suttle

*Finally, be ye all of one mind, having compassion one of another, love as brethren,
be pitiful, be courteous: Not rendering evil for evil, or railing for railing:
but contrariwise blessing; knowing that ye are thereunto called, that ye
should inherit a blessing. For he that will love life, and see good days,
let him refrain his tongue from evil, and his lips that they speak no guile:*

1 Peter 3:8-10

As a Christian, our life's purpose is to honor and glorify Christ and to point others toward our Savior. In order to achieve this, our goal should be to seek to become more like Him everyday. In order to become more like Him, we should seek to know His heart and mind! How we act, how we treat people, and how we speak is a huge part of how others see Jesus through us!

In these verses, we get a quick picture of how our speech should be according to His heart: compassionate, loving, thoughtful, and kind. We should not snap back to unkindness, instead we should respond with kindness. The passage goes on to make clear that this is not just a suggestion but rather a command to be followed in order to receive the blessing of God. Verse ten sums it up by saying, if you want to be blessed, do not speak evil. I do not think many of us are tempted to have evil conversations about sin, but if we are living in the flesh, it can be easy to speak evil by putting others down or speaking negatively of them.

I Corinthians 15:33 says, "Be not deceived: evil communications corrupt good manners." Sometimes we will justify our negative speech about someone else as "a prayer request," or even say that we were helping to build that person up by bluntly telling them how they need to improve. But in reality, was it truly necessary?

When I read these verses, it encourages me to always respond with kindness and encouragement. It encourages me to always think and speak the best of people. If you live this as a rule, you will be surprised by how much joy this adds to your life! You will enjoy being around people more because you will see the best in them and how they are a part of God's blessing in your life. People will enjoy being around you more because they know they will leave encouraged in Christ! Take this challenge to speak an encouraging word to someone in your life today. Use your words to build people up and point them to the Lord.

words

Thoughts:

Prayers:

Dealing with Hurt and Adversity

By Renee Patton

...pour out your heart before him....

Psalm 62:8b

Have you been hurt? Have you received man-induced adversity? I know, who hasn't? We have all been hurt at one time or another. At a time in my life when hurt was at its height, God gave me a timely message to hear. This particular Sunday morning I was home, and my church was having issues with the Livestream, so I pulled up another preacher I enjoy hearing. I believe the connection trouble was meant just for me because I needed to hear how to manage my hurt.

In Psalm 62-69, David is reaching out to God, both in admiration and frustration. David begins by stating his confidence in God (vs. 1-7). Then, in verse eight, David knows he must pour his heart out to God. David knows God will take care of others who cause the hurt we feel

It may be that
I must walk
through fire
and water;
but God will
be with me
every step
of the way!

(vs.12). In Psalm 63, David expresses a longing for God and glorifies Him for His goodness. Psalm 64 brings a prayer for deliverance. "They search out iniquities..." (6a) and "...God shall shoot at them with an arrow; suddenly shall they be wounded" (vs. 7). This is where it seems clear that David knows adversity has been thrown to him by his enemies. God will take care of others who bring adversity; however, it does not seem so, yet vengeance is God's, not mine. This is a statement I must repeat at times in my life. It seems natural to want to lash out to others who bring pain, although it is not mine to give.

In Psalm 65, David asserts God's power and goodness and follows up in chapter 66:12b with "...we went through fire and through water: but thou broughtest us out into a wealthy place." I have to remember God will deliver me. It may be that I must walk through fire and water; but God will be with me every step of the way! FIRE equals hurt & anguish; PAIN during FLOODS may cause me to lose sight which equals DROWNING. My focus must be God!

David knows God's blessings will come, and God is his Source of strength (Ps. 67-68). Finally, in Psalm 69, David's humanity is shown at something to which we can all relate! David begs for God's help, "Save me..." (vs. 1a). I am drowning, Lord, save me! I cannot stand! I cannot see! I need Your deliverance! We have all been there! Feeling overwhelmed with hurt or adversity, the water is so high we cannot even walk. Drowning is the only relevant emotion.

Then others noticed David was not himself in verse eight. How often do we see this in others or even ourselves? In verse 20a, David states, "Reproach hath broken my heart; and I am full of heaviness...." About one week before hearing this message, I said to my husband, "I just feel so heavy!" Now, David's harsh reality – David asks God to choke them (vs. 22), make them blind (vs. 23), deliver His wrath to them (vs. 25), dish out double iniquity and do not allow them in His presence (vs. 27), and finally, David wishes they were not even born (vs. 28).

The constant high and low of David during these verses relates to each of us. God, You are merciful, but these people Lord! And God, You are so good to me, but these people Lord! These are feelings we all have. During moments of pain or hurt, we have thoughts that need to be brought into subjection. So, cry out to God! Cry so hard your eyes hurt and your mouth is dry. Get up, blow your nose, wipe your face, and move forward. Express your pain to God, or you will express it to others. God makes a way to achieve victory – we must pour out our hearts to Him!

words

Thoughts:

Prayers:

Sticks and Stones

By Stephanie Young

But the tongue can no man tame;
it is an unruly evil, full of deadly poison.

James 3:8

How many times have we heard the saying, "Sticks and stones may break my bones, but words will never hurt me"? What a false statement! A cut or bruise will heal with time, but words spoken can pierce the heart and can never be taken back or may never be forgotten.

In Proverbs, we find that our words can:

- Make a glad heart — Proverbs 12:25
- Turn away wrath — Proverbs 15:1a
- Be as honeycomb: sweet to the soul and health to the bones — Proverbs 16:24

Or our words can:

- Stir up anger — Proverbs 15:1b
- Cause wounds — Proverbs 26:22

In the church, we find people from all different walks of life. Each person is so different, yet with the Lord's help, we can work together in unity to spread the light of the gospel in our communities. One of the easiest ways to break that unity is with our words.

James 3 explains just how powerful our tongue is. Verse 8 says, "But the tongue can no man tame; it is an unruly evil, full of deadly poison." We must attempt to tame our tongue, and it must be a non-stop effort on our part. When our tongue is tame, we will only speak words that will be helpful and constructive to those that hear them.

Our words can display to this world the joy and love that only God can give, or it can display the deadly poison spoken of in James 3. How do we speak to our family? Many times, we are not as cautious with our words around those we love the most and feel the most comfortable around. How do we speak when we are in public? Do people notice us being grumpy and discontent? Or will they see us being joyful and loving even in a difficult situation? Make your words count for Christ.

words

Thoughts:

Prayers:

Clapping Your Way Up the Steps

By Alycia Cruse

*In every thing give thanks: for this is the will of God
in Christ Jesus concerning you.*

1 Thessalonians 5:18

Over one Christmas holiday, my husband and I traveled back to our hometown where we stayed with his family for a couple of days. What was once four families with many children (and I mean many—my husband's family alone had ten children!) has now become large branches of children's children with ever-expanding life paths.

While we were there that week, our baby decided she had the courage to learn a new skill—climbing the stairs. It first started with just the two small stairs leading into the living room. Her determination was strong and before long she was not satisfied with the two little stairs. She turned her sights to the bigger ones.

I heard what sounded like little hands clapping and an ever-so-sweet voice say, "Yay!" Then silence again. Suddenly, the clapping again and the tiny, "Yay!"

I thought it was so odd so I started looking to see where she was. Sure enough, she had made it halfway up the stairs going to the second story. I was terrified. But my little baby was so happy to see that her mom had come to see her progress. Her clapping and celebrating got even louder. Up the next step she went. The soft tiny voice was now a resounding "YAY!" It was contagious so I celebrated with her! I began clapping my hands and copying her happy voice.

Motivated, she went up the next step with ease — only one left until she reached the landing! By this time, the noise of our celebration brought two more people to investigate. They were shocked to see their baby sister had made it up the stairs, and she was so excited to see them. She celebrated again by clapping her hands and squealing with delight. Her brother and sister came down to hug and praise her success.

Wow. I was struck. How many times do we see a brother or sister in Christ on our social media pages celebrating the blessings of God in their life, and we give into feelings of jealousy, bitterness, or maybe even anger? We hear word of a family member who gets a new promotion, or is able to purchase a new car, and instead of being happy for them, we recluse into our own pain and shut them out.

Even deeper, how do I treat the small victories and blessings God sends my way? Can I praise Him alone? Without anyone cheering me on? Praise produces faith. Praising God for blessings demonstrates the faith to believe they came from Him. James 1:17 says, "Every good gift and every perfect gift is from above, and cometh down from the Father of lights, with whom is no variableness, neither shadow of turning."

If a brother is blessed, praise God! If you are struggling to reach the top and feel you will never get there, praise Him for each small blessing and clap your way up the steps.

words

Thoughts:

Prayers:

Don't "Pass it On"

By Coretta Gomes

She openeth her mouth with wisdom; and in her tongue is the law of kindness.

Proverbs 31:26

We have all played the game "Pass it On," or as some may call it, the "Telephone Game." It is loads of fun, yet it holds an invaluable lesson and alarming truth. What gets repeated does not always come out as what it was meant to be.

The seriousness of our words was once again brought to my mind when we recently played this game at a church gathering. The leader told the first person a funny sentence, which was not quite coherent, then it was repeated down the line to four other people. (Granted the four others all had noise mufflers on and had to read lips.) However, by the end of the game, they had only gotten two words right. The original message was totally lost. We laughed and laughed from the outcome.

Unfortunately in life, it is not usually a laughing matter and ends up hurting or alienating the very brethren with whom we one day will spend eternity. Proverbs 26:22a says, "The words of a talebearer are as wounds ...". The saying, "sticks and stones may break my bones, but words can never hurt me" in reality is not true. Words hurt and cause wounds! The hurt might heal through forgiveness and much prayer, but just like wounds, they take time to heal and generally leave scars.

We all struggle with our words and need to be careful what we repeat to others. Even words that are not harmful, when repeated over and over again, can come out wrong. Years ago at our church, there was a person-to-person prayer line. Each member of the church was in charge of getting the prayer request out to two or three other members. In one instance, the one needing prayer ended up deceased by the time the prayer line had gotten to the last person! Needless to say, nowadays we have a recorded phone service. They laugh and joke now about how they "killed off so and so," but in reality, even things that are not gossip sometimes get all jumbled up in the end.

Before getting together with others, make it a habit to pray that the Lord will help you be careful with your words. Keep in mind Proverbs 26:20, "Where no wood is, there the fire goeth out: so where there is no talebearer, the strife ceaseth." When around those who casually mention, "Have you heard about...?" Instead of giving a listening ear, say "Let's pray for them and let God take care of it." Do not be the one to fuel the fire!

Proverbs 31:26 says, "She openeth her mouth with wisdom; and in her tongue is the law of kindness." The Bible has much to say about our words because it is a powerful tool. So let us be careful about how we use our words as they do affect other people!

words

Thoughts:

Prayers:

Words of Effect

By Misty Wells

He that hath knowledge spareth his words: and a man of understanding is of an excellent spirit. Even a fool, when he holdeth his peace, is counted wise: and he that shutteth his lips is esteemed a man of understanding.

Proverbs 17:27-28

There has never been, nor will there ever be, a more effective Speaker than the God of all creation. His words are so powerful that, out of nothing, light is spoken into existence, a firmament is put in place, and heaven and earth are created. He speaks and the earth brings forth grass, the herb yielding seed, and fruit trees yielding fruit after their kind. He said "Let there be lights in the firmament of the heaven..." and a black night is filled with breathtaking bursts of light that have been burning for thousands of years, all a result of His effective words (Gen. 1). After the work is complete, He makes a small statement about the outcome of what He has spoken —it is good. His Words are life giving, true, and direct. They always fulfill their purpose.

It is evident in the Word of God that quantity is never equal to quality. The Lord did many great things through mere Words, and often His

Words were few. Someone once said that women speak about 20,000 words a day, close to 13,000 more than the average man. Wow! We have a lot to say. With all the talking that is taking place, how truly effective are we with our words? Furthermore, what kind of effect do our words have? Is your conversation full of simple fillers that waste time and cause others to cringe when you begin? Or are they limited in number and great in purpose? The Bible says in Proverbs 17:27-28, "He that hath knowledge spareth his words: and a man of understanding is of an excellent spirit. Even a fool, when he holdeth his peace, is counted wise: and he that shutteth his lips is esteemed a man of understanding."

May our words be few, but full of knowledge and understanding. May they build up and not break down. My hope is that you take time to consider before you speak. I challenge you today to accomplish something great with what you say. Be effective with your words!

words

Thoughts:

Prayers:

Lord, Save Me

By Anonymous

*But when he saw the wind boisterous, he was afraid;
and beginning to sink, he cried, saying, Lord, save me.*

Matthew 14:30

Save me. I have prayed this prayer in the quiet of my room. I have called out these words through a broken heart and angry tears. Sometimes, Satan has a way of making your life fearful by causing doubt. He throws those hurt feelings in your path. He plants bitterness way down in your heart. He makes the unknown future look terrifying. Sometimes, the only words I can utter when I am overwhelmed by the storm, sinking in fear, and losing my faith are, "Lord, save me."

Peter said it in Matthew 14:30, " But when he saw the wind boisterous, he was afraid; and beginning to sink, he cried, saying, Lord, save me."

David said it in the following verses:

- Psalm 109:26 - "Help me, O LORD my God: O save me according to thy mercy."
- Psalm 6:4 - "Return, O LORD, deliver my soul: oh save me for thy mercies' sake."

133

- Psalm 69:1 - "Save me, O God; for the waters are come in unto my soul."
- Psalm 71:2 - "Deliver me in thy righteousness, and cause me to escape: incline thine ear unto me, and save me."
- Psalm 3:7 -"Arise, O LORD; save me, O my God: for thou hast smitten all mine enemies upon the cheek bone;"

Let the pain in your heart cause you to cry out to God for strength. Let Him reach out to you as He did with Peter in Matthew 14:31. Let Him give you His Words of wisdom during a time when your words are inadequate. When you are afraid and overwhelmed, cry out, "Lord, save me."

Sometimes, the only words I can utter are , Lord, save me!

words

Thoughts:

Prayers:

Which Woman's Words Will You Choose?

By Marissa Patton

Every wise woman buildeth her house:
But the foolish plucketh it down with her hands.

Proverbs 14:1

I was convicted as I began to study Proverbs. I quickly found that there are two women whose words have an effect — one woman leaves destruction (Proverbs 22:14, 23:27, and 14:1b), and one woman elicits praise (Proverbs 31:28-31). Although I may not use my words in the same context as this destructive or "strange woman," I do not want to use them in any way that would reflect her and her actions. I would rather elicit praise. Let's take a look —

The Destructive Woman

She flatters. Read Proverbs 2:16, 6:24, 7:5, and 26:28. According to Webster's Dictionary, to flatter means "to praise excessively especially from motives of self-interest." The strange woman used flattery to draw attention to herself. I must be careful to make my conversations with others genuine and draw the attention back to Christ, otherwise, I may be "working ruin" with my words.

She has fair speech. See Proverbs 5:3-8 and 7:21. Basically, she is a "smooth talker." She uses her tone of voice to deceive. Ever met someone that can cover any mistake they make with quick talking and a white lie? This woman used her fair speech deceitfully and ruined lives as a result. No way do I want to speak like that!

She frustrates. This is the one that convicted me the most, particularly in the area of my marriage. Check out Proverbs 19:13, 21:9, 25:24, and 27:15. Why would I want a marriage where my husband would rather live on the rooftop than be around my constant nagging ("continual dropping") and argumentative words ("contention")?

She is flamboyant. Read Proverbs 7:11-12, 9:13-15, and 11:22. We can be so over-the-top sometimes. Clamorous means "loud and noisy." The word "stubborn" is mentioned in those verses also. Are we quick to argue and voice our opinion? Are we that person who never can see the other side of a situation because we are too stubborn to show humility? This woman was calling to strangers and discontented with her own home. I want to have a "meek and quiet spirit" as mentioned in I Peter 3. Hypothetically, I want to build my home, not leave it to ruin while I chase after other endeavors that may pull me away from Christ.

I would rather be like the woman in this verse – "Every wise woman buildeth her house:..." Proverbs 14:1. Proverbs 31:25-26 says, "Strength and honour are her clothing; And she shall rejoice in time to come. "She openeth her mouth with wisdom; And in her tongue is the law of kindness." Not only does she live a life of rejoicing, wisdom, and kindness, but at the end of Proverbs 31, we see those around her are praising and blessing her with their words! This is the woman whose words I want to pattern my life after. What about you? What words will you choose?

words

Thoughts:

Prayers:

About The Authors

Each author has been handpicked because of their testimony
of Christ. God has gifted each writer with incredibly versatile
perspectives of the Christian life. These godly ladies come from
all walks of life including pastor's wives and daughters,
missionary wives, church staff ladies, and faithful church
members. Their written words of wisdom are sure
to bless your heart.

To know more about our writers please visit:
thehighlyfavouredlife.com/our-story

Salvation Made Simple
By Renee Patton

Admit. One must first admit they are a sinner. Romans 3:10 states, "As it is written, There is none righteous, no, not one." Sin is everywhere and we all commit sin, many times without even trying. Perhaps in a conversation, we say something innocently, then realize it was not correct. That, my friend, is lying. Of course, murder is a sin that is seen and felt by those affected. However, lying is too. Jeremiah reminds one that "The heart is deceitful above all things, and desperately wicked: who can know it?" (17:9). A baby does not have to be told how to sin, it is simply in our nature. One must admit they are a sinner otherwise we make God a liar as found in I John 1:10, "If we say that we have not sinned, we make him a liar, and his word is not in us."

Believe. One must believe Jesus came to this earth to be born and die for our sins. "For God so loved the world, that he gave his only begotten Son, that whosoever believeth in him should not peish, but have everlasting life" (John 3:16). God desires that we should not perish, thus the choice is ours. God gives man the opportunity for salvation if man would take it. Romans 5:8 states "But God commendeth his love toward us, in that, while we were yet sinners, Christ died for us." Webster's 1828 Dictionary defines commendeth as entrusts or gives. So, God gave us His love through His Son, Jesus. Furthermore, Romans 5:19 shows how sin came from Adam and is made righteous through Christ, "For as by one man's disobedience [Adam] many were made sinners [mankind], so by the obedience of one [Jesus] shall many [mankind] be made righteous."

Confess. Confession is made with one's own mouth. The words must come from the person alone. Romans 10:9 talks of both confession and believing, "That if thou shalt confess with thy mouth the lord Jesus, and shalt believe in thine heart that God hath raised him from the dead, thou shalt be saved." The key is I have to confess to God. My husband or friend cannot confess for me. While God gives man the opportunity on earth, there will be a time every knee will bow and confess God is Lord, "For it is written, As I live, saith the Lord, every knee shall bow to me, and every tongue shall confess to God" (Romans 14:11).

To see more resources on salvation visit:
https://www.thehighlyfavouredlife.com/simple-salvation

If you made this decision, please contact us at *highlyfavouredlife @gmail.com*. We would love to rejoice with you in the new life you now have in Christ.

143

prayer

A Highly Favoured Life Devotional

Check Out
The Highly Favoured Life
on

and
thehighlyfavouredlife.com

www.ingramcontent.com/pod-product-compliance
Lightning Source LLC
Chambersburg PA
CBHW060325050426
42449CB00011B/2650